Lost
in Boston

Also by Jane R. Wood

Voices in St. Augustine

Adventures on Amelia Island:
A Pirate, a Princess, and Buried Treasure

Trouble on the St. Johns River

Ghosts on the Coast:
A Visit to Savannah and the Low Country

Lost in Boston

Jane R. Wood

Jane R Wood

Florida Kids Press ◆ Jacksonville, FL

Publisher's Cataloging-In-Publication Data
(Prepared by The Donohue Group, Inc.)

Wood, Jane R., 1947-

Lost in Boston / Jane R. Wood.

pages : illustrations ; cm

Summary: The Johnson family travel to Boston from their home in Florida to attend a cousin's wedding. While there, they visit a number of historic sites. Suspense and intrigue only add to the family's adventure in this historic town.

Interest age level: 008-014.

Issued also as an ebook.

ISBN: 978-0-9863325-0-0

1. Historic sites—Massachusetts—Boston—Juvenile fiction. 2. Families—Massachusetts—Boston—Juvenile fiction. 3. Boston (Mass.)—Description and travel—Juvenile fiction. 4. Boston (Mass.)—History—Juvenile fiction. 5. Historic sites—Massachusetts—Boston—Fiction. 6. Families—Massachusetts—Boston—Fiction. 7. Boston (Mass.)—Description and travel—Fiction. 8. Boston (Mass.)—History—Fiction. I. Title.

PZ7.W664 Lo 2015

[Fic]   2014922097

Library of Congress Control Number: 2014922097
Cover design and graphic design by Elizabeth A. Blacker
Cover image: iStockphoto.com/Jorge Salcedo
Published through:
Florida Kids Press, 11802 Magnolia Falls Drive
Jacksonville, FL 32258
904-268-9572

www.janewoodbooks.com

Printed and bound in the USA.

*To those teachers who make American history
exciting for young people.*

Acknowledgments

I love visiting historic places, so taking my characters to Boston was a real treat. Many people helped make that happen.

My sister Priscilla Beckman, who traveled with me to Boston, and my cousin Kristi Caruso, who lives near Boston, were both helpful in identifying appropriate locations for my readers.

I received valuable input from professionals at several historic landmarks in Boston, including Patrick M. Leehey, Research Director at the Paul Revere House; Erin Wederbrook Yuskaitis, Director of Education at the Old North Foundation; and Kate Monea, Archivist at the USS Constitution Museum. Thanks also to Mike's Pastry in the North End, for allowing me to feature their store in the book, and to Mike Carpenter, who shared details about attending a Red Sox game at Fenway Park. Thanks to David Coviello and the Paul Revere Memorial Association for the use of their photographs.

Special thanks go to fourth-grade teacher Linda Smigaj, who is National Board Certified in Literacy; children's author, Frances Keiser; copy editor, Beth Mansbridge; and graphic designer, Elizabeth Blacker—all of whom provided their expertise to help me polish, edit, and format this book.

As with all my books, I owe a great deal of gratitude to my husband, Terry Wood. His constant support makes it all possible for me.

Chapter 1
Going to Boston

Four suitcases, three backpacks, a large purse, and Winnie-the-Pooh. They were all loaded into Jennifer Johnson's minivan, along with her three kids—Joey, Bobby, and Katy. The kids' grandfather was driving them to the airport so they could catch a plane to Boston.

"I know I've forgotten something," Jennifer Johnson said, glancing behind her to the backseat.

"Aw, Mom, you always say that," fourteen-year-old Joey said. "If we've forgotten anything important, we can buy it in Boston."

"That's easy for you to say," she said. "Remember, we're on a budget."

They had been invited to the wedding of one of Jennifer's cousins who lived about an hour outside of Boston. Jennifer had decided to take the whole family so they could meet some of their relatives, and also do some sight-seeing in Boston.

Jennifer loved history and whenever possible she planned trips to historic places so her kids would also gain an appreciation for their heritage. They had visited other historic towns, such as St. Augustine, considered the Nation's Oldest City; Savannah, Georgia; and Charleston, South Carolina—all within driving distance of their home in Jacksonville, Florida. But they had never been to the New England area, "where our country was born," as Jennifer told her kids.

Since they were going to be studying about these places in school, she wanted them to see the cities in person.

"It will be so much more meaningful for you when you read about these places, after you've been there," she said.

"Whatever," ten-year-old Bobby said. "I'm just glad we get to miss three days of school."

Bobby was in middle school and played on the school baseball team. The school's baseball season was already over so he wouldn't miss any games. He also knew they would probably go to Fenway Park, as his older brother was a huge Boston Red Sox fan.

"Mom, did you order some tickets online for a game?" Joey asked his mother.

"No, dear. But I don't think that will be a problem. Someone else is taking care of that for us," she said.

Joey was especially excited about the trip. He was going to connect with a girl he had met more than a year ago when her family was on vacation in Florida. He and Barby had been emailing each other ever since. They were both freshmen in high school now, and they always had plenty to talk about. He was concerned that she might have grown taller than him. *That would be embarrassing*, he thought.

When they arrived at the airport, they checked their bags at curbside so they wouldn't have to carry them inside. The kids were given their backpacks and six-year-old Katy tucked Winnie-the-Pooh under her arm. Their grandfather gave each of the kids a hug and a ten-dollar bill.

"Buy something fun," he said. "Have a good time and be safe."

As they walked through the airport, their mother reminded them to stay together so they wouldn't get lost.

"Airports are very busy places, so you need to pay attention to where you're going," she said. "I put our travel itinerary with all our flight information and my cell phone number in each of your backpacks. If you get separated from us, go to one of the official airplane counters and tell them you're lost. They'll call me or make an announcement so we can find each other."

"Maybe you should put a leash on Bobby, because he always wanders off," Joey said.

"Very funny," Bobby replied. "Just give me a map and I can find my way anywhere. I have superior navigation skills."

"Well, navigate yourself through security so we can get to the gate," Jennifer said. "We don't want to miss our flight."

They passed through security without setting off any blaring alarms—and Winnie-the-Pooh got a free X-ray.

Chapter 2
Fasten Your Seat Belts

Because they were a family traveling with children, they were allowed to board the plane early. They had four seats together, but Joey and Bobby were across the aisle from their mother and Katy. Before they put their backpacks in the overhead compartments, each of the kids selected something to read or play with during the flight. Joey was rereading *Johnny Tremain*, a book that both he and Bobby had read in the fifth grade. The story takes place in Boston during America's struggle for independence. Bobby was playing with his electronic game, and Katy had a coloring book and crayons.

Joey said, "Bobby, you should read this again because you'll be studying more American history in the eighth grade. We'll see many of the places mentioned in the book, like the Paul Revere House and the Old North Church."

In planning their trip Joey had studied several Boston websites to help decide what places they should visit.

Because they only had two days scheduled for sight-seeing, he wanted to make sure they went to the places that he had read about and studied in school.

"I like the part in the book where Johnny Tremain gets to listen in on the meetings of the Sons of Liberty," Joey said. "Meetings like that actually happened. Those men, like Sam Adams and Paul Revere, were really brave. They could have been arrested by the British soldiers and hung for being traitors to the king."

Bobby said, "I liked the part where Johnny delivered coded messages to members of the Sons of Liberty, and when he spied on some of the British officers."

"Yeah, he knew the British soldiers wouldn't pay much attention to young people, like the stable boys and the girl servers in the pubs, so the kids often overheard military plans that could be shared with the Patriots, who were trying to figure out what the British were going to do next," Joey said.

"Joey, do you think you'd have the courage to spy on someone if it was dangerous?" Bobby asked.

"I don't know. It would depend on the circumstances and how dangerous it was."

"Yeah, me too. I guess we won't know until we find ourselves in that kind of situation."

They were both thinking about that as the plane engines roared and they started to taxi down the runway. Katy was squeezing Winnie-the-Pooh tightly. Jennifer patted her on the leg and assured her that everything would be OK.

Soon the flight attendants offered them soft drinks and snacks.

"Free Coke and pretzels," Bobby said. "I think I'm going to like traveling by airplane."

"Don't get used to it, because it's expensive," their mother said.

"Mom, you forget. I'm going to be a millionaire when I grow up. I'll own my own plane—maybe two."

"Have you figured out how you're going to do that?" Jennifer asked.

"No, but I'm working on it," Bobby said as he popped a pretzel into his mouth.

Chapter 3
Tunnels and Traffic

After they had landed at Logan Airport in Boston and were making their way through the terminal, they were surprised to hear so many different languages being spoken by people walking by.

Bobby nudged Joey on the arm when a man wearing a turban passed them. "We're not in Kansas anymore, Toto," Joey said, quoting a line from *The Wizard of Oz*.

They collected their luggage at the baggage claim area, and were shocked at how much cooler the weather was than in Florida. Every time one of the exit doors opened, a blast of cold air came rushing in, making them shiver.

"I'm glad we all packed jackets," their mother said. "We might even get some rain."

"Was I supposed to bring a jacket?" Bobby said.

"Yes, you were. It was on the list I gave you of things to pack," she said. "But just in case, I checked everyone's bag before we left, and I put one in your suitcase."

9

"Thanks, Mom. You think of everything."

"I try to. I hope I can find my cousin among all these people. Kristina said she'd meet us here at the baggage claim area."

Just then a blond woman came rushing toward them.

"Jennifer, yoo-hoo. It's me, Kristina." She threw her arms around their mother and gave her a big hug. "I think it's been eighteen years since we saw each other last. You haven't changed a bit."

"I've changed a little. I now have three kids," Jennifer replied with a chuckle. "And here they are."

Jennifer introduced each of them to her cousin.

Kristina shook their hands and said, "Welcome to Boston. I hope you'll enjoy your visit here. We probably need to get a move on, as the traffic is terrible in the afternoons. Plus, my kids will be home from school by the time we get to the house, and they're eager to meet their Florida cousins."

She guided them to the parking garage and loaded their luggage into the back of her SUV.

"My kids have some DVDs back there, if you want to watch a movie," she told the kids.

"No," Jennifer said, "I'd prefer they look out the windows and see some of Boston."

That wasn't a problem. The kids were mesmerized by what they saw. As they left the airport, dozens of cars were trying to merge into two lanes that led into a tunnel. The sounds of traffic and honking horns were all around them.

"Everyone, make sure you have your seat belt on securely," Kristina said. "The drivers here can be a little aggressive."

Two of the cars in front of them were merely inches apart, both trying to merge into the same lane at the same time. Kristina honked her horn, while staying close on the bumper of one of them.

Bobby and Joey exchanged looks and grinned at each other. Katy closed her eyes and turned Winnie-the-Pooh's face into her chest so he wouldn't be scared. When she opened her eyes again a few seconds later, it was dark.

"What happened?" she asked.

"We're in the Ted Williams Tunnel that goes under the Boston Harbor."

Joey perked up. "Ted Williams was a famous Red Sox player."

"You're absolutely right," Kristina said. "I heard you were a Sox fan."

"Miss Kristina, did you say we're going under the water?" Katy asked. "What happens if there's a leak?"

11

"Hopefully, that won't happen," Kristina said as the returning daylight made them squint. "Now, the challenge is to get out of this city traffic and onto the interstate as soon as possible."

Everyone was quiet as Kristina zigzagged through several city streets. They saw many tall buildings and what seemed like hundreds of pedestrians rushing along the sidewalks.

"We're going to take the Massachusetts Turnpike that goes past Fenway Park. And over that way is the North End. I'm sure you'll want to go there."

"Isn't that where Paul Revere's house is?" Joey asked.

"That's right. You know your history, don't you?"

Jennifer told her cousin that Joey had done some research on Boston when they were planning their trip. She explained that she wanted the kids to see some of the historic sites. Because they only had two days to do that, she had asked Joey to find a part of the city where they could see the most in a short amount of time.

"Then the North End is a great place to go. You'll be able to walk part of the Freedom Trail," Kristina said. "And they have great Italian restaurants there. The pizzas are delicious, and you'll have to get a cannoli."

"What's a cannoli?" Bobby asked. "It sounds like a vegetable."

"No, it's not a vegetable—and I guarantee you, you're going to like it."

As they stopped for a red traffic light, a large vehicle that looked like a military truck of some sort pulled ahead of them in the left lane.

"What the heck is that?" Bobby said.

"That's one of the duck tours. They're very popular," Kristina said. "They're actually recycled amphibious landing vehicles from World War II. They give tourists a tour of the city and then drive right into the Charles River for a panoramic view of the Boston skyline."

When the light changed, Kristina pulled up alongside the multicolored vehicle. She rolled down the window on that side of the car and told the kids to wave to the people in the strange-looking truck. When the kids waved at the tourists, they were greeted with a chorus of loud quacks from the occupants.

"That's so cool," Bobby said. "Can we take a duck tour?"

"Probably not this trip," their mother said. "We'll put it on the list of things we want to do when we come back."

Kristina steered her way to the interstate, and they left the noisy city of Boston behind.

14

Chapter 4
It's All Relative

They traveled on Interstate 90 for awhile, and then they drove along a two-lane road that took them through several small picturesque towns. The houses looked different from the ones in their Florida neighborhood. Most of them were two stories tall and many of them had white picket fences or rock walls outlining their yards. The trees were different too—no palms.

"What are those trees with the white flowers?" Katy asked.

"They're cherry blossoms," Kristina said. "They always bloom this time of year. You'll notice some cherry trees with light pink blossoms and others with dark pink ones. It's a sign that spring is coming."

"Kids, you'll see lots of things that are different from where we live," Jennifer said. "That's why I like to travel—to learn about other places, how other people live, how things are different, and ways that we're all alike."

"Speaking of how things are alike, you can now meet your cousins,"Kristina said. She pulled in to a driveway."I think you'll find that you have many things in common."

They had arrived at a large two-story white house with black shutters. A three-car garage was loaded with bicycles, soccer balls, ice skates, hockey sticks, lacrosse equipment, and an array of athletic shoes.

"How many kids do you have?"Bobby asked.

"Only two boys, but my husband and I are pretty athletic too,"Kristina said.

As the kids got out of the car, Katy wandered over to the silver ice skates that were dangling from a hook."I've never been ice skating before,"she said."Can we go?"

"We have some indoor skating rinks, but I don't think we'll have time to do that this weekend,"Kristina said."Get your mother to bring you back someday and I'll take you there myself."

They gathered their suitcases and backpacks and headed into the house. Kristina showed the boys where they'd be sleeping, in bunk beds in one of her boys' rooms, while Katy and her mother would be in the guest room.

Kristina gave them a tour of the house, showing them a large playroom for the kids. It had no furniture in it except for a large-screen TV at one end of the room and a bookshelf loaded with board games. The floors were carpeted and there was more athletic equipment stacked in one corner.

"My boys play all kinds of games in here, including soccer. You kids make yourselves at home. My kids should be home from school any minute now."

Just then, they heard the back door close with a loud slam.

"Mom, we're home," a young voice yelled.

"We're up here. Come meet your cousins from Florida."

Two boys, one blond and one with brown hair, scrambled into the room. The blond boy was taller and looked a lot like his mother. His name was David and he was in the sixth grade. The younger boy was Alan. He was in the fourth grade.

"This is Joey, Bobby, and Katy, and they're going to be staying with us for several days," Kristina said. "Why don't you kids get to know each other, while their mother and I begin making dinner?"

Alan started kicking a soccer ball around, and soon Bobby was passing it back to him. David turned on the TV, looking for the Red Sox game.

"I'm a Red Sox fan myself," Joey said. "I think we're going to go to a game while we're here."

"Yeah, I heard my mom and dad talking about getting tickets. I think we're going too," David said. "Have you ever been to Fenway?"

"No, and I can't wait to go."

David told Joey that his family goes to a Sox game several times a year. "It's like a family tradition," he said.

"We take a family picnic to the beach every year for our family tradition," Joey said. "My grandparents come with us and we have a rip-roaring game of kickball on the beach."

"We do that too, sometimes—not on the beach, but in the backyard," David said. "I guess our families are a lot alike."

"Hey, you guys want to play soccer in the backyard?" Alan said. "We can probably get a game in before dinner."

Because the Red Sox game was almost over and they were losing, Joey and David agreed. Katy said she would not play with them because she didn't want to hurt any of them.

Joey and Bobby grinned.

"You'll get used to my little sister," Joey said. "Sometimes she's a little sassy."

"I'll take that as a compliment," Katy said, prancing out of the room to join the ladies in the kitchen.

Leading the other boys downstairs, David said, "You'll get to meet another one of our cousins—actually, your cousin too—and she's a lot sassy."

"Girls are silly," Alan said.

Bobby and David agreed, but Joey followed them in silence.

Chapter 5
Ducks and Swans

The next day, Kristina drove the Johnsons into Boston so they could take one of the trolley tours of the city.

"I'm going to take the scenic route along the Charles River and hopefully we'll see some crew teams practicing," she said.

Bobby asked, "What are crew teams?"

"It's a very popular sport here. Many schools and colleges have crew teams that compete against each other. Maybe you've seen them in the Olympics," Kristina said.

They spotted several long, skinny boats skimming across the water. Some of them had two people in them and some had eight people, all rowing in sync with each other.

"Those boats are called racing shells, or sculls," Kristina said. "The rowers in the sculls need to synchronize their oars so they move quickly and efficiently across the water."

"I'd like to do that someday," Bobby said.

"We actually have some rowing clubs at home," Jennifer said. "See, you've already discovered a whole new sport you didn't know about."

Kristina took a right turn off the busy thoroughfare and pulled up in front of a large park. She gave Jennifer a map and told them she'd pick them up in the same spot around five o'clock.

"This is the Boston Public Garden. I know there's something you want to see in there," she said, with a wink to Jennifer. "The Boston Common is across the street. That's where the Visitor Information Center is located. You can purchase your tickets for the trolley tour there. You've got my cell phone number if you have any questions or you get lost."

"We'll be fine, I'm sure," Jennifer said. "Thank you for driving us into the city."

As Kristina drove away, Jennifer gave instructions to the kids, reminding them to stay together and not wander off.

"Bobby, you stick close to Joey; he has his cell phone with him. I'll keep Katy with me … and speaking of Katy, we're going to start the day off with a special surprise for her."

She took Katy's hand and headed into the Boston Public Garden. They walked down a sidewalk that meandered

22

past colorful flower beds filled with red tulips and yellow daffodils. They had walked only a short distance when Katy started to run, pulling her mother along with her.

"The ducklings!" she squealed. "I always wanted to see them. That's one of my favorite stories."

She hopped up on the back of a bronze duck statue that was almost as big as she was. Behind the large duck trailed eight smaller ducklings.

"I remember that book—*Make Way for Ducklings*," Joey said as he and Bobby caught up with them. "Isn't that where the mama duck decides to build her nest in the middle of a city park?"

"Yes," replied Jennifer. "And this is that park. Right over there is the island where the ducklings were born."

Katy skipped down the line of ducklings, patting each one on the head. Other children were petting the shiny statues while parents snapped photographs. Jennifer took a picture of Katy sitting on Mrs. Mallard.

"We'll have to print a copy of this and frame it for your bedroom," Jennifer said. "Let's walk over to the lagoon. There's something else I want you to see."

Katy gave the mama duck one last hug and joined her mother and brothers as they strolled toward the water. They saw statues and fountains and a bridge that led to a small island. Jennifer pointed out the pedal-powered swan boats. Each boat had a large white swan on the back. Katy, however, was more interested in the real swans that were gracefully gliding near a weeping willow tree.

"Aren't they beautiful!" she exclaimed. "This is like being in a fairy tale. Swans and daffodils and weeping willows. I love Boston!"

"I'm glad you're enjoying this, but we need to move on if we're going to see more of the city," her mother said.

They walked across the street to the Boston Common, another large park located in the center of the city. They passed a group of schoolchildren on a field trip. Their guide, dressed in a colonial costume, was explaining that the Boston Common is the oldest public park in the United States.

The guide said, "The early residents let their cattle graze here, as it was a common area for all to use. And British troops camped here before the Revolutionary War."

"Can you imagine having cows in the middle of a big city?" Bobby said. "That had to add all kinds of interesting sounds and smells."

"That was in the 1600s and 1700s, before it was a big city," Jennifer said. "A lot of what you're going to see in Boston goes back more than three hundred years. Let's buy our tickets for the tour, and if we have time before the next trolley arrives, I want to visit a graveyard that's near here."

Bobby nudged Joey and said, "Graveyards! People are dying to go there."

"Bobby, that's such an old joke."

"Yeah, but it's still funny."

Chapter 6
Old Granary Burying Ground

Jennifer purchased their tickets for the trolley tour at the Visitor Information Center, and then directed her kids over to the Old Granary Burying Ground located in the next block. She told them many of the Revolutionary War heroes are buried there, including Samuel Adams, John Hancock, and Paul Revere.

"I want to see Paul Revere's grave," Joey said. "C'mon, Bobby, let's go find him."

The gray headstones were lined up in neat rows, though many of them were leaning at crooked angles and some were covered in moss. A 25-foot-tall obelisk in the center of the cemetery marked the grave of Benjamin Franklin's parents. Victims of the Boston Massacre were also buried there.

Jennifer and Katy caught up with the boys, who were talking about Paul Revere.

"He lived to be eighty-four years old," Joey said. "Just think of all the changes he saw in his lifetime."

"Many of the men buried here played significant roles in our country's history," Jennifer said. "I wanted us to pay our respects to the people who shaped our nation."

As they left the burying ground, Jennifer explained that much of what they would see is part of the Freedom Trail, a 2.5-mile walking route that weaves past many historic sites. The trail is marked by a line of red bricks in the sidewalk.

"You mean we're going to walk for two and a half miles?" Bobby asked.

"No, that's why we're taking the trolley tour. It will give us a good overview of the city," Jennifer said. "There's no way we can see it all in two days, and this tour will let us hop off and back on at different locations if we want to spend any time at the stops."

They arrived at the trolley stop the same moment as a large bus pulled up to the corner. Jennifer showed the driver their tickets as the kids scrambled to find two seats together.

"Welcome aboard," the driver said when his passengers were settled down. "My name is Joseph and I'm going to drive you around our fair city and share some of its history. Let me know if you have any questions and I'll try to answer them for you." He pulled the vehicle into the street.

Bobby whispered, "Can I ask him why they call this a trolley tour when it's actually a bus?"

"No, that would be rude," Joey said.

"That building on our left with the gold dome is the Massachusetts State House," the driver said. "The original dome was made out of wood, but it leaked. So in 1802, Paul Revere's company covered it in copper. Now it's gilded in gold leaf. Our governor has his office in that building, and that's where our state legislature meets."

Joey said he wondered why they didn't name the city after Paul Revere, adding, "He seems to be everywhere."

As they drove past the waterfront area, the driver told them about the Boston Children's Museum, the New England Aquarium, and the floating Boston Tea Party Museum. Before they had the chance to ask, Jennifer explained to her kids that they'd have to save those places for a future visit. Their first stop was at Quincy Market, a historic marketplace that today houses many shops and places to eat.

"Let's get off here for an early lunch," Jennifer said. "I'd like a lobster roll. They have all kinds of food, so everyone can have what they want."

They walked through the crowded food court, eyeing the wide variety of foods being sold. They saw seafood and clam chowder vendors, as well as Italian, Mexican, Indian, Greek, and Chinese cuisines. The aromas created by the international foods attracted many tourists. Donuts, cupcakes, and gelato got Bobby's attention.

Katy and Bobby decided to split a pizza, and Joey joined his mother for a lobster roll. They took their food outside and ate on a bench, where they did some serious people-watching. When they finished eating, they walked across the courtyard to Faneuil Hall, a four-story brick structure with a grasshopper weather vane at the top. They eavesdropped on a tour guide who was describing the history of the building to some senior citizens.

"Faneuil Hall has been a meeting hall and marketplace since 1742. Samuel Adams made some of his most passionate speeches in this building. There's a statue of Adams on the other side of the building. The meeting hall on the second floor is still used today for government functions and many politicians have made important announcements from there," the tour guide said.

He explained that the grasshopper weather vane has become a symbol for the city of Boston. During the American Revolution, suspected British spies were asked what was on top of Faneuil Hall. If they could not identify the grasshopper weather vane, they were convicted of being a spy.

"That's cool," Joey said. "It sounds like something out of a spy movie."

"Are we going to go inside?" Bobby asked.

"We can if you want to, but remember we only have a few hours. I was hoping we could tour the USS *Constitution* today, which I thought you might find more exciting," Jennifer said.

Joey asked, "Isn't that the ship called 'Old Ironsides'?"

"That's it," Jennifer said. "It's the oldest commissioned warship still afloat in the world today."

"Well, let's weigh anchor and set sail for the *Constitution*," Bobby said.

Chapter 7
"Old Ironsides"

They hopped back on their tour bus, which took them over to the Charlestown Navy Yard. Because the USS *Constitution* is a fully commissioned US Navy ship, they had to go through a security check. All visitors over the age of eighteen had to show a valid photo ID.

When they left the ship's security entrance and got their first full-length view of the ship, they were amazed. The massive black ship was more than three hundred feet long from stem to stern.

"I had no idea it was so big," Joey said.

"It's awesome," Bobby said. "I wish I could sail on it someday."

A woman in a naval uniform came up behind him and said, "Maybe you can. Have you ever thought of joining the Navy?"

"Actually, no. I'm just a kid, you know. But I can't wait to get on board," Bobby replied. "Do you work here?"

"Yes, I'm stationed here. I'm a sailor in the US Navy," the woman said.

Katy tugged on her mother's sleeve and whispered to her, "She's a woman. I thought sailors were men."

"There are many women in the military today—and in lots of other jobs that used to be limited to men," her mother replied. "When you grow up, you can do pretty much whatever you want to do."

Katy thought about that as they walked toward the ship. "That's good to know. There are lots of things I want to do."

"I know what I want to do," Bobby said. "I'd like to climb up one of those masts or fire a cannon. Now, that would be way cool."

The sailor told him there would be no climbing up the mast, but if he wanted to hear a cannon fired, he'd have to be there in the morning when they'd raise the national flag, or at sunset when they'd retire it for the night. They also fire the cannon on the Fourth of July when the ship sails into the harbor and on other special occasions, she said.

As they walked up the steep gangplank, they heard another sailor giving a brief talk about the historic warship. He told the small crowd of tourists that the USS *Constitution* was built in Boston, named by President

George Washington, and launched in 1797. They learned it was originally commissioned to protect American merchant ships from Barbary pirates, but earned its name of "Old Ironsides" during the War of 1812.

"One of the reasons America declared war on England in June of 1812 was because British warships were seizing American ships," the sailor said. "In August, *Constitution* encountered the British frigate, the HMS *Guerriere*, off the coast of Nova Scotia. During the sea battle between the two vessels, cannonballs shot from the HMS *Guerriere* bounced off the planking of *Constitution*, causing very little damage. One sailor shouted that her sides must be made out of iron, and that's how she got the name 'Old Ironsides.'"

The sailor led the group of tourists several feet along the open deck before he stopped and turned to them. "When *Constitution* fired her cannons on the broadside of the HMS *Guerriere*, much of the enemy's rigging was cut away. The battle lasted only thirty-five minutes," the sailor said. "'Old Ironsides' accumulated a 33-0 battle record between 1797 and 1853."

"That's like batting a thousand, in baseball terms," Bobby said to his family. "No wonder she's so famous."

The sailor told them the Navy maintains the famous warship to educate the public on America's maritime heritage and to preserve an important icon of American history. She's like an ambassador who honors the many sailors and marines who have served our country, he said.

Katy asked him if the ship was really made out of iron.

He told her no. The hull was constructed of several kinds of pine and oak, with the hard and resilient woods coming from the states of Maine to Georgia. He said its design was cutting-edge technology for the time when it was built, making it especially strong—like iron.

"And Paul Revere created the copper fastenings for the frigate," he told them.

"It sounds like Paul Revere's influence was here too," Joey said.

They walked the length of the deck, marveling at the rigging on the three masts. The tallest mast reached more than two hundred feet into the sky. A sailor was explaining to some visitors how the short-range cannons on the spar deck worked.

"If you'd like to see more cannons, go below, to the gun deck," he said. "Watch your step going down the steep ladders. Another sailor will be giving a tour down there."

They gingerly climbed down a ladder that led to the deck below. They saw a long line of cannons on each side of the ship. A row of cannonballs was lined up neatly, and the well-worn wooden floors displayed a nice shine. Another sailor was giving a talk about the history of the warship, with detailed descriptions of some of her battles.

"I can't believe how big it is," Bobby said.

"And it's so shiny everywhere," Katy said. "They must really polish it a lot."

The female sailor they had met earlier was standing near the captain's quarters. She said, "I'd be glad to answer any questions you have."

"How many people did it take to sail this ship?" Joey asked.

She told them the ship originally sailed with four hundred to five hundred men aboard, including some young boys who acted as officers' servants. These boys helped keep the officers' uniforms and cabins clean, served them dinner, and sometimes carried powder to the guns during battle. They were expected to learn as much as they could about seamanship, she said.

"We have records of one young boy, David Debias, whose father signed him up as a cabin boy at the age of eight. He earned $31.98 for seven months of service in 1815," she said.

"You've got to be kidding!" Bobby said. "We made more than that in a few hours when we held a car wash."

"Times were different then," Jennifer said. "Hopefully, learning things from the past will help you understand and appreciate what many people—even the young people—had to go through years ago."

"I'm glad I live today, and not back then," Bobby said.

The sailor smiled at him and said, "Today the ship maintains a crew of about seventy. They are responsible for conducting the tours, participating in official ceremonies, and maintaining all the parts of the ship. You're lucky you're here now. She's going into dry dock soon, and will be there for several years."

They toured the captain's quarters and walked around the ship some more. Because it was overcast and looked like it was going to rain, Jennifer suggested they return to the bus so they wouldn't get wet.

As they were leaving the ship, Bobby said he thought this was one of the coolest places they'd ever visited.

"Thanks, Mom, for bringing us to Boston. I can't wait to tell my friends about this really neat lady I met on our trip," he said with a chuckle.

"Don't you think she's a little old for you?" Joey said.

"She may be more than two hundred years old, but she sure is beautiful!" Bobby said.

Chapter 8
Back to the Present

They boarded their tour bus again as it was starting to sprinkle.

"I'm glad we toured the *Constitution* before it started raining," Jennifer said. "I think we'll stay on the bus for the rest of the afternoon."

Joey was disappointed when the bus driver told them they wouldn't be able to go by Fenway Park because there was a game that day and there would be too much traffic. They drove through the Back Bay neighborhood, known for its many three- and four-story brownstone houses. They saw tall, modern skyscrapers like the 52-story Prudential Tower, and older classic buildings like the Boston Public Library, which is the second-largest library in the country.

The tour guide pointed out Trinity Church, considered a masterpiece of American architecture. It was known for its beautiful stained-glass windows, massive tower and big arches, and rough stone exterior, he said.

"I love all these different kinds of architecture," Jennifer said. "I'd like to write a story about each one of these buildings."

Jennifer Johnson was a freelance writer who wrote stories for magazines and newspapers.

"Maybe we'll have to come back to Boston so you can do some research," Joey said. "I really like this place and wish we could stay longer."

"Me too," Bobby said. "I'd like to go back to the *Constitution*. Maybe Grandpa can come with us next time. He likes all that history stuff."

"I know for a fact he'd like it. Your grandfather was in the Navy when he was a young man," Jennifer told them. "You should ask him to tell you about his experiences. Then you'll have a personal connection to the past."

Everyone was quiet and lost in thought as the bus meandered its way back to the Boston Common. As they were getting back to the place where they had boarded the bus, Jennifer asked each of her kids what they thought about Boston.

Katy said she like the ducklings. Bobby said it was hands down the USS *Constitution*. He said the next time he had to do a history report for school, he'd write about that ship.

"Bobby, that makes this whole trip worth it," his mother said. "Anything to get you excited about history makes my day."

Joey said he was eager to visit the North End, so he'd save his opinion for tomorrow.

As they exited the bus, Katy thanked the driver and added, "You drove safely and I liked all the things you said."

"Thank you, young lady. I hope you enjoy the rest of your visit to our fair city," the driver replied.

"People here are nice," Joey said. "I hope we can come back someday."

They walked to the place where Kristina had left them that morning. It was almost five o'clock when Jennifer's cell phone rang and she laughed as she said that would be OK.

"Kristina is stuck in traffic and will be about thirty minutes late. She suggested we take a stroll through Beacon Hill, which is across the street from here," she said. "It's one of the most historic residential areas of Boston. I'd love to see some of the houses."

They wandered down Charles Street, which housed restaurants, boutiques, and shops selling antiques, art, and home furnishings.

"Let's cross over to one of the streets that's more residential," Jennifer said. "Beacon Hill is a National Historic

41

District. It's known for its brick sidewalks, gas street lamps, decorative ironwork, flowering trees, and brick row houses. Many famous people have lived here over the years, and some still do."

Joey said, "This is like some of the homes we saw in St. Augustine, Savannah, and Charleston."

"That's right," Jennifer replied. "Many communities see the value of preserving their historic structures. In fact, the architecture of these homes is protected. If you bought one of these houses, you would have to get approval to make any visible changes to the outside of the building."

"That doesn't seem fair," Bobby said. "If you buy something, you ought to be able to do what you want with it."

"Bobby, I kind of like these old buildings," Joey said. "Besides, if they didn't save them, we wouldn't be here today looking at them, and you'd be home doing homework right now."

Bobby thought about that for a moment. "I see your point. These old houses are beginning to grow on me."

Jennifer checked her watch and announced that they needed to return to the Public Garden so they could meet Kristina. As they crossed Beacon Street, they saw Kristina waving to them.

"Did you guys have a good day today?" she asked as they scrambled into her SUV.

Bobby and Katy started talking at the same time, sharing their excitement about what they had seen.

"Sounds like it was a good day," Kristina said, laughing. "How about you, Joey?"

"I liked it too, but I'm really looking forward to going to the North End tomorrow. I have a feeling that's where my journey will get really interesting."

Chapter 9
Dozens of Cousins

Back at Kristina's house, they met more relatives they didn't know they had. Many of them had arrived for the cousin's wedding which was going to take place Saturday evening. The bride and groom were there, as well as many other adults.

After everyone was introduced, the kids were told they could go upstairs to the playroom. Another boy about David's age, named Timothy, and a tall girl, Sarah, who looked like she could be in high school, were the only other young people there.

Katy asked the girl her name and how old she was. The girl responded that her name was Sarah with an "h" and she was sixteen.

"My brother is fourteen, but he has a girlfriend," Katy said.

"That's a relief," Sarah replied. "I'm not in the market for a boyfriend right now."

Joey was embarrassed by Katy's comment, so he pretended he didn't hear what they were saying. "Is there a Red Sox game on today?" he asked David.

"They're usually night games on Fridays. The game won't start for another half hour," David said. "Why don't we play a board game or a card game until then?"

"I can play Crazy Eights," Katy said with enthusiasm.

That did not seem to be a popular choice with the boys. Sarah said she'd play Crazy Eights with Katy and the boys could do what they wanted. Alan suggested they go outside. Joey said he had to make a phone call.

In a teasing tone, Bobby announced: "Joey's got a girlfriend."

Joey ignored him as he left the room.

An hour later, everyone was called to dinner. The smells coming from the kitchen were mouth-watering. The dining room table was loaded with salads, all kinds of vegetable dishes, fried chicken, homemade bread that Kristina's mother had baked earlier, and a variety of desserts including brownies, cookies, and a chocolate cake. The bride and groom were allowed to serve themselves first, as the guests of honor.

When Jennifer had finished eating, Joey said he needed to talk to her. He wanted to know what the plans were for

Saturday. Jennifer told him that one of the relatives worked at Harvard and offered to drive them there in the morning, and they could catch the T at Harvard Square that would take them into town. Kristina had told Jennifer she would be busy with wedding preparations, and riding the subway system, known as the T, would be a true Boston experience for the kids.

"Actually, that sounds great," Joey said. "I talked to Barby on the phone and she would like to go with us tomorrow. She knows all about the Freedom Trail and has offered to show us around."

"Sounds like a plan," Jennifer said. "Although we have to return in time to get ready for the wedding tomorrow evening. Remember, that's why we came here. I'd like you to go look at some of the photo albums that Aunt Susan brought. There are some interesting ancestors on our family tree."

"I'll do that. But first I gotta go call Barby and see if she can meet us at Harvard Square."

As he stepped outside to telephone Barby, he saw Bobby, David, and Alan climbing a tree in the backyard.

It made him think about his family's branch of the family tree. Would future generations be talking about them? Would Bobby, Katy, and he make any serious contributions to their country, like Benjamin Franklin or Sam Adams or Paul Revere?

He'd have to think about that tomorrow, when they were visiting one of the places where it all began. Right now, he was trying to focus on making an important phone call.

Chapter 10
Saturday Surprises

Barby was waiting for them near the T entrance in Harvard Square. She had grown taller since last summer, but Joey was relieved to see that she wasn't taller than he was; he had also grown several inches. Katy ran to her and gave her a big hug. Joey held back, feeling awkward. Jennifer also hugged her and asked about her parents.

When all the greetings were over, Barby smiled at Joey and said she was glad they came to Boston. She said she had been looking forward to seeing him again. He blushed and said he was glad to see her too.

Barby asked if they had ever ridden a subway before. Only Jennifer had. She said they'd have to walk down the stairs to enter the subway. It would be noisy and crowded, with people rushing everywhere. Barby cautioned them to stay together and not get separated. Jennifer clasped Katy's hand and warned Bobby to pay attention. Barby explained that they could buy their tickets from a machine.

"I've got a CharlieCard, so I don't need a ticket," Barby said.

"What's a CharlieCard?" Bobby asked.

"It's a card that I buy in advance and then swipe it at the turnstile to enter where the tracks are. You'll see lots of people using them. It saves time and money," she said. "You'll only be riding the subway for one day, so you can purchase individual tickets." She showed Jennifer how to purchase the tickets—enough for four of them to go inbound to the city, and four for their return trip.

"Why do they call it a CharlieCard?" Katy asked.

Barby explained that it was named for a man in a song that was popular many years ago. A man named Charlie got on the train and while he was riding it, the fare went up and he'd have to pay an exit fee to get off. He didn't have any money with him, so he had to ride the train forever. The song says "he's the man who never returned."

"What happened to him?" Katy asked with concern.

"It's just a song. There was no Charlie. But people in Boston liked it, so they named the card after Charlie, as a tribute to him," she said. "If everyone is ready, let's head downstairs."

As they entered the underground tunnel, she pointed to a large map on the wall with different colored lines going in several directions.

"We're going to take the red line inbound, and change to the orange line going to Haymarket. That's the closest stop to the North End. I've got a map here that shows all the stops. It's fairly simple to use. If you want to go somewhere, you find the name of the stop where you want to go and catch that colored line to get there. It makes it easy to get around, and we don't have to worry about any traffic jams in the streets because we're going under them."

Katy was nervous as they approached the turnstile. Barby flashed her card over an electronic reader, and instructed them to put their tickets into a slot which would open the turnstile for them to go through. The boys did that easily, and Jennifer helped Katy with hers.

They waited on the platform for their train. A man with a bushy black beard and a baseball cap was playing a saxophone near the stairs that were leading to another platform. Occasionally, someone put a few coins in a cup he had set in front of him.

As the red line train made its loud whooshing appearance, they felt a rush of wind come surging through the tunnel. When the train stopped, the doors opened and a group of noisy kids loaded down with backpacks pushed their way through the door and hustled up the exit stairs.

"Let's go," Barby said as she headed for the door. "Try to find some seats together."

They hurried onto the train, Barby leading the way. She found three empty seats together, and signaled for Jennifer and Katy to sit in them. Joey suggested she take the third seat, saying he and Bobby could stand.

"Hold onto the strap above your head or hold onto one of our metal bars. We've got several stops before we change trains, and it's very easy to lose your balance when the train starts and stops."

The train started to move.

A tall man wearing a dark blue Yankees T-shirt bumped into Bobby as he walked by. "Watch it, kid," he said.

A boy about Bobby's age mumbled an apology to Bobby as he passed.

"What did you say?" the man said to the kid. "You don't go apologizing for me. You hear me?"

"Yes, sir," the boy said.

"Go find a place to stay outta my way."

The boy slipped onto a seat near the back of the car. He stared at the floor and didn't say another word.

Jennifer asked Bobby if he was OK. He said he was.

Bobby asked Barby if it was OK for Joey to take a picture of him on the train with his cell phone. He said he wanted evidence to show his friends that he rode the subway, a form of transportation not available in Florida. Joey said it would make them look like tourists, but when Bobby pointed out that they were tourists, Joey reluctantly agreed.

Joey waited till the train stopped at the next station so the photo wouldn't be blurry from the train's rocking motion. He took a picture of Bobby standing in the aisle. He took another one of his mother and Katy, and then one of Barby, who smiled up at him.

Little did he know that his picture-taking would become a different kind of evidence later that day.

Chapter 11
The North End

After successfully changing trains, they arrived at the Haymarket stop. Barby led them through a park and over to Hanover Street. She explained that the North End is known for its Italian food and feasts.

"Because it's such a pretty day, it will soon get very crowded," Barby said. "Let's go to the Paul Revere House first."

The sidewalks were sprinkled with pink blossoms falling from the cherry trees that lined the streets. Several store owners were unrolling awnings that covered the fronts of their shops. Many of the restaurants were open to the street, showing tables covered with white tablecloths ready for hungry customers. Some of the cafés had colorful flower boxes outside and displayed menus offering a variety of pastas and pizza.

An elderly couple passed by them, speaking Italian.

"Those people talk funny," Katy said to her mother.

"No, dear. They're speaking Italian," Jennifer said. "They probably moved here from Italy many years ago. Boston was settled by immigrants from many different countries, and as Barby explained, many of the people who came from Italy settled here."

"I bet they make good pizza here," Bobby said.

"Yes, they do," Barby said. "We can get some for lunch, but first let's get a little history."

She led them down a side street, following the red brick path in the sidewalk indicating the Freedom Trail. They turned onto a cobblestone street and came to a small park known as the North Square. A few benches faced a gray, two-story wooden structure.

"There it is," Joey said. "I want to take some pictures before we go in."

"We'll go sit on one of those benches while I tell Katy and Bobby about Paul Revere," Jennifer said.

Jennifer explained that Paul Revere was one of the Sons of Liberty, a secret group of Patriots that was formed to protect the rights of the colonists from the British government. The king of England was imposing taxes and laws upon the American colonies, but the colonists had no say in how they were governed. Their motto was "No taxation without representation."

The king sent British troops to occupy Boston in order to maintain control over the colonials, she said. On the evening of April 18, 1775, the Patriots realized that the British troops were going to march to Lexington to arrest Samuel Adams and John Hancock, two outspoken members of the Sons of Liberty. The army troops also planned to seize the weapons that the colonists had hidden near there, in Concord.

Paul Revere had to sneak out of town in a rowboat, borrow a horse in Charlestown, and ride to Lexington to warn the colonists that the British were coming. Another rider, William Dawes, took a different route to Lexington that night, making sure one of them was able to alert the others. After warning the citizens of Lexington, the two riders connected with a third rider, Dr. Samuel Prescott, on their way to Concord. They were captured by British soldiers for a short period, but were then released. Because the colonists were aware that the British soldiers were coming, they were prepared to meet them.

When the British arrived in Lexington, a small skirmish occurred and several colonials were killed. Another battle at Concord's North Bridge became known as "the shot heard round the world," because that was the beginning of the American Revolution and our country's road to independence from England, Jennifer told them.

"They were very brave men," Barby added. "They could have all been arrested and hung as traitors to the king. Also, most of the colonists who fought against the British troops were farmers and shopkeepers, not professional soldiers. I'm always amazed when I think how courageous they were. If it hadn't been for them, we might not be the United States of America today.

"This was the house that Paul Revere left from on that historic night," Barby said. "Some of the furnishings in this house were owned by his family. It also displays some of his silver. Paul Revere was a talented silversmith."

Courtesy, Paul Revere Memorial Association

"Yeah, we heard that he made part of the dome on the Massachusetts State House and some of the copper fastenings on the USS *Constitution*," Bobby added.

They studied the house that was built in 1680. Its windows had diamond-shaped panes of glass, and its second floor was hanging over the first floor slightly, in the style of that period.

Joey had finished taking his pictures and signaled to the others that he was ready for the tour. They entered into the courtyard located on the side of the house and purchased their tickets.

The first room they visited was the kitchen. They saw a large brick fireplace with several cast-iron pots hanging from a metal arm that could swing over the fire. Bundles of herbs were hanging from the mantel that held several pewter plates and other household items. A work table, a baby's cradle, and a rocking chair also occupied the room. The wooden floors creaked as they passed into the next room.

Touring the house, they read the information panels that explained many of the home's features. They learned that this building was the oldest remaining structure in downtown Boston. Paul Revere had purchased the house in 1770 and lived there with his first wife, and then his second wife, his mother, and some of his sixteen children.

The second floor contains the main bedroom. One wall is painted a pale yellow and the others are covered with blue wallpaper. A large canopy bed occupies the center of the room. Candlesticks and washbasins remind visitors of the way people used to live.

"It must have been hard to try to work or read by candlelight," Joey said. "And I can't imagine not having running water."

"It's not very big for such a large family," Katy added.

"It was actually quite spacious by 18th-century standards," Barby said. "Every time I visit a historic house like this, I like to imagine what it was like to live back then."

"I like to pretend too," Katy said excitedly. "I'm glad you're taking this tour with us. Boys just don't get it."

Jennifer called for Katy to join her in the next room.

Joey leaned closer to Barby. "Thank you for making her feel special," he said. "I was afraid all this history would be a little boring for her."

"No problem. I like her," Barby said. "And I kind of like her oldest brother too."

Joey smiled and said, "He kind of likes you too."

"You actually said you like me?" Barby said. "Now, that's a historic moment. Paul Revere would be proud," she said as she strode away.

Joey shook his head. *I wonder if girls were that sassy in the 1700s,* he thought.

"I have a feeling some things never change," he said to himself, and he joined the others.

Chapter 12
Pizza and Paul Revere

"I'm starving," Bobby said. "Can we get some pizza?"

The streets were more crowded when they finished their tour of the Paul Revere House. They walked back to Hanover Street and found a restaurant that had an empty table. After ordering two kinds of pizza, Jennifer pulled some papers out of her purse and started to read in a theatrical voice:

"Listen, my children, and you shall hear

Of the midnight ride of Paul Revere,

On the eighteenth of April, in Seventy-five;

Hardly a man is now alive

Who remembers that famous day and year."

She paused to make sure her kids were listening. Joey and Barby were laughing; Katy was spellbound; and Bobby glanced around to see if other people were looking at them.

"Mom, you're embarrassing us," Bobby said.

"No, no, go on," Katy begged.

Jennifer continued.

> "He said to his friend, 'If the British march
> By land or sea from the town to-night,
> Hang a lantern aloft in the belfry arch
> Of the North Church tower as a signal light,—
> One if by land, and two if by sea;
> And I on the opposite shore will be,
> Ready to ride and spread the alarm
> Through every Middlesex village and farm,
> For the country folk to be up and to arm.' "

A man sitting at the table next to them said, "That was delightful! I haven't heard that poem since elementary school. Henry Wadsworth Longfellow, isn't it?"

"Yes, that's correct," Jennifer said. "It's the beginning of 'Paul Revere's Ride' and it was published more than eighty years after his famous journey through the countryside. In fact, it was Longfellow's poem that made Paul Revere even more celebrated. However, I'm told some of the details in his poem are not totally accurate. Longfellow liked to write lyrical poems about history and legends."

The lady sitting with the man said, "And so appropriate for where we are today. I hope you children appreciate all the history you're seeing here."

"Yes, ma'am," Joey said politely.

Barby said the next place they would visit was the Old North Church, where the signal was given from the belfry tower.

"You'll see exactly where the lanterns were hung so the Sons of Liberty could 'spread the alarm … to every village and farm …,'" she said. "The signal from the church tower was sent to indicate that the British troops were going to travel by land or by sea to get to Lexington and Concord."

"Because they didn't have cell phones back then, they had to figure out a way to send a message from across the river without the British knowing," Joey said. "That was brilliant."

"I'm kinda proud of the old guys," Bobby said. "That would make a good spy story."

"It actually is a *real* spy story," Jennifer said. "There are other books you should read that tell of the many daring deeds that took place during this early period of our country's history. Lots of secrecy, bravery, and perseverance. We owe those Patriots a lot."

The kids were quiet, thinking about what it must have been like in 1775. The silence ended when bubbling hot pizzas were placed on the table.

Katy said, "I wonder what kind of food the early settlers ate?"

"I'm sure there are cookbooks that feature dishes from that period," Jennifer said. "Let's look for one and then we can make some of the recipes when we get back home."

"They have a great gift shop at the Old North Church," Barby said. "I bet you can find one there. They also have a good selection of kids' books."

"I've already read *Johnny Tremain*," Bobby said. "I liked that one. Kids actually did some undercover work in that story. Maybe I'll use some of the money Grandpa gave me to buy another book."

"Can I get a book?" Katy asked. "Grandpa gave me some money too."

"I think that would be a great way to spend your money, and I know Grandpa would like that," Jennifer said. "Now let's eat so we can tour the Old North Church and get back to Kristina's in time to dress for the wedding."

As the kids finished the pizzas, Jennifer asked the waitress for their bill. The waitress told her that the couple sitting next to them had already paid it. Jennifer turned to the man to thank him.

"We're just trying to spread a little Boston hospitality," he said. "I hope you and your family will visit us again."

"Why, thank you," Jennifer said. "That was very nice of you."

"It was our pleasure," he said, and the woman nodded in agreement. "The poem you read about Paul Revere brought back some wonderful memories. We can see that you're creating some good memories too."

"I hope so," Jennifer said. "That's why we came on this trip. It looks like the kids have decided that we will be coming back again someday."

"That's what we like to hear," the lady said. "I hope you enjoy your visit to the Old North Church."

Their visit to the historic church would prove to be memorable in many ways.

Chapter 13
The Old North Church

They posed for pictures in front of the Paul Revere statue. Joey also took a photo that showed Paul Revere on his horse, while capturing the steeple of the Old North Church in the background.

"This will be my artsy shot," he said to Barby.

"You really like taking pictures, don't you?" Barby said. "I thought you were into writing."

"I like doing both," he said. "Plus, the pictures help me remember what I saw. If I want to write about it later, I have the photographs to remind me of many of the details that I might have forgotten."

As they slowly walked toward the historic church, they talked about what they would like to be when they grow up. Both agreed they wanted to go to college after high school.

"I don't know what kind of job I'll get, but I hope it will involve some kind of writing," Joey said.

"I'm a science person," Barby said. "I know girls aren't supposed to like math and science, but I guess I broke the mold. Sometimes I'm kind of feisty too. I'll probably end up in a few controversies."

"That's not all bad. Wasn't the American Revolution a controversy in its day?"

"For sure. Thank you for pointing that out. I guess that's why I like to study about people who had to fight for what they believed in."

"Me too," Joey echoed. "Their bravery continues to amaze me. It's one thing to read about it in a book, but to see where it actually happened makes a much bigger impression."

"Are you serious about coming back again someday?" she asked.

"Definitely. I might even look into applying to some colleges up here," he said.

"That's funny, because I was thinking about applying to some schools in Florida."

They looked at each other and laughed.

"What's so funny?" Bobby said as he fell in step beside them.

"We were talking about how funny you are," Joey said.

"Would that be good funny or bad funny?" Bobby asked.

"Good funny, of course," Barby quickly replied before Joey could say something else.

"I'm glad to know that I am appreciated," he replied. "You never know when I'm going to do something truly amazing."

"Oh, good grief," Joey said. "I'm amazed you haven't gotten lost since we've been here."

"The day's not over yet," Bobby replied.

They walked around to the front of the church, but had to wait while a group of noisy students on a class field trip exited through the front door. When the Johnsons and Barby entered the church, they were surprised by the stark white walls that seemed even brighter because of the large clear glass windows. One of the Old North Church educators announced she would be giving a short presentation in five minutes if they would like to move to the front.

As they walked down the center aisle, Joey said, "I expected stained-glass windows. And there are no rows of pews like in churches today."

"That's because this is a very old church. In fact, it's the oldest church building in Boston," said one of the guides. "Back then churches built box pews, a tradition brought with them from England. These cubicles allowed families to sit together, and also protected them from drafts on cold winter mornings. Sometimes people would place hot coals or bricks in metal foot warmers on the floor to add some warmth, and often families would decorate their pew boxes with furniture, cushions, fabrics, and even wallpaper."

The guide told them they could sit in one of the box pews while they listened to the presentation. They selected a box near the front.

The speaker shared details about the founding of the church, its architecture, and the role it played in the American Revolution. She also told them about the

church's caretaker, Robert Newman, and John Pulling Jr., who are credited with sending the signal to the Patriots in Charlestown by lighting two lamps in the church steeple.

"That was an act of bravery, as not only did the Patriots see the signal, but the British troops did, as well," she said. "Legend tells us that Newman had to rush down the stairs of the eight-story steeple and jump out a window as British soldiers were knocking on the church's door that night. That window over there is known as the 'Newman window,'" she said, pointing to the right of the altar.

"Now, that's the kind of history I like to hear," Bobby said when the woman was done speaking. "Can I walk around and explore a little? I won't leave the building."

Jennifer nodded and reminded him not to touch anything. She, Katy, and Barby wandered through the sanctuary, admiring the brass chandeliers and the four wooden cherub statues that flanked a huge pipe organ on the second floor at the back of the building. Joey was busy taking pictures.

When they were ready to go to the gift shop, they realized Bobby was not in sight.

"I told you he'd get lost," Joey said.

"No, I'm sure he's here," Jennifer said. "He told me he would not leave the building. We need to find him, though."

They discovered him in one of the box pews, talking to a boy about his age. Because they were sitting down, it was hard to see them over the box wall.

"Bobby, we've got to go," Joey said. "Mom and Katy want to visit the gift shop, and we still want to get a cannoli before we head back."

Bobby said good-bye to his friend.

"That's the same kid who was on the T with us this morning," Bobby said. "He's here with his uncle, but I don't think he likes him very much. He was trying to hide from him. His uncle is from New York and is taking care of him while his mom is out of town."

"You need to be careful," Joey said. "His uncle was kind of a jerk. You need to stay away from people like that."

Far away, Bobby thought.

But that was not to be.

Chapter 14
Chaos in the Gift Shop

"I love this place," Barby said as they entered the gift shop. "I always find the neatest things in here. There are all kinds of souvenirs, jewelry, T-shirts, photographs, artwork, and a good selection of books."

"I'm going to look for a cookbook," Jennifer said. "Katy, you come with me and then we'll go find the picture books."

Bobby headed back to the book section. Joey followed Barby, who was looking for a charm for her bracelet. A school group entered the store, creating a great deal of commotion.

Bobby noticed his new friend, Josh, was there too. Josh's uncle was pushing his nephew against the wall and telling him he better do what he was told, or else he'd be sorry.

Bobby also overheard him say, "We'll meet at that old cemetery on Copp's Hill, up the road, when you've got it."

When Josh's uncle walked away, Bobby went over to Josh to ask if he was OK. He could tell Josh had been crying.

"He wants me to steal something over there," Josh said. "He said he'd cause a distraction so I can get out of the building with it. My mom would be very upset if she knew what he was making me do."

"You shouldn't have to do that," Bobby said. "Let me get my mom. She'll know what to do."

Just then, a tall boy with the school group came running through the store, chasing one of his friends. He bumped into Josh, who fell against a book stand that tipped over, spilling books across the floor. One of the store clerks hurried over to Josh as the teacher from the group pursued the two boys.

Joey and Barby rushed back to where Bobby was standing.

"What happened?" Joey asked. "Did you do that?"

"No, it was some kids from that school group," he said. "But I need to find Mom. We've got a problem."

Bobby helped Josh get up.

Josh looked around to see where his uncle was. "Oh no," he said. "He just grabbed a wallet out of that purse sitting by the cash register."

Within a couple seconds, the uncle had walked out of the store while everyone was focused on the chaos in the back of the store.

The teacher returned to the cash register and screamed, "Someone stole my wallet!"

Josh ran after his uncle.

Bobby told Joey that it was the man on the T who stole the wallet, and he was heading to a cemetery near there. "I'm going after Josh. He needs help."

"Bobby, don't!" Joey screamed.

But it was too late.

Chapter 15
Bobby to the Rescue

Bobby sprinted out of the gift shop a few seconds before a police officer appeared and locked the door. He announced that no one was to leave the building.

"We've got to tell my mom," Joey said to Barby. They rushed over to the cookbook section.

"What was that all about?" Jennifer said. "And where is Bobby?"

"Mom, Bobby saw that man who was on the T this morning—the one who pushed Bobby. He said that boy saw the man steal a woman's wallet," he said. "Bobby and the boy who was with that man ran after him when he left the store. The police have locked the building, but we need to go after Bobby. That man is dangerous."

"Come on, we need to talk to the police," Jennifer said with concern.

Holding Katy's hand, Jennifer pushed through the crowd so she could get to the police officer. Many of the other adults who were with the school group had gathered around the teacher whose wallet was stolen.

"Excuse me," Jennifer said, "but my son knows who stole the wallet. Please let us through."

The officer asked her to step aside from the crowd so they could talk.

"Are you with the school group?" the officer asked.

"No. But my son knows who took the wallet. Joey, tell him what happened."

Joey told the officer about the man from the subway. He told him that the man took the wallet and left the building, and then the man's nephew ran after him.

"My brother had made friends with the nephew," Joey said, "so he ran after him. Bobby heard the man say they're supposed to meet up at a cemetery near here."

"You mean Copp's Hill Burying Ground?" the officer said.

"If that's near here, then I think that's it," Joey said. "We have to go after my brother. That man could hurt him because he can identify him."

"Can *you* identify him?" the officer asked.

"Not really. He was tall and wore a Yankees shirt."

"Wait a minute," Barby said. "You have a photo of him on your cell phone. Remember when we looked at the pictures you took on the T this morning, you commented that you got that man in the background."

"That's right," Joey said. He turned on his cell phone and scrolled through his pictures. "Here it is. That's the guy," he said, pointing to the man's picture.

The officer studied it for a minute, and then stepped away to talk into a walkie-talkie.

When he walked back to them, he said, "We've got an officer near Copp's Hill. I've given him a description of the man. Hopefully our thief is still in the area. Will you send that photo to my phone? We can use it as evidence."

Joey sent the photo to the police officer. "Can I get out of here? I need to go find my brother," Joey said.

Jennifer was not happy with that comment. The police officer stepped away again and took a phone call.

"Mom, I need to go!" Joey pleaded. "We can't stand here and do nothing."

"You won't have to," the officer said when he returned. "The man you identified has been apprehended and he still had the stolen wallet in his possession. We think this guy has a history of stealing from tourists."

Joey jumped up and yelled "Yes!" He gave Barby a hug, and asked the officer if he could go now.

"I'll unlock the door, but check with your mom before you go running off," he said. "The Copp's Hill Burying Ground is up Hull Street, in front of the church. You can't miss it. Now I have to go calm down that hysterical woman."

Joey asked his mom if he could go find his brother. Jennifer said she'd be right behind him, but moving a little slower because of Katy.

"Oh, by the way," the officer said, turning back to Joey. "You and your brother showed a lot of courage today. Your mom and sisters should be proud of you both. I've got your phone number from when you sent me the photo. We'll call you if we have any questions."

Joey grinned, and then said to Barby, "He thought you were my sister too."

"Fat chance," she said. "But I'm proud of you too!"

"C'mon, let's go find *our* brother," he said with a laugh.

84

Chapter 16
Copp's and Cops

Joey and Barby raced up the hill. They saw a police car with its blue lights flashing, and two police officers talking to Bobby and Josh, who were sitting on the curb outside the entrance to the cemetery.

Bobby waved to his brother when he saw him.

"Are you OK?" Joey said.

"Yeah!" Bobby said. "But I don't think Josh is doing so great."

Josh was staring at the ground. One of the police officers was talking to someone on his cell phone, and then he handed the phone to Josh.

"Mom, I'm sorry," he said, and started sobbing. "He wanted me to help him steal things."

A long silence followed while Josh listened to his mother, often shaking his head in agreement. When their conversation was over, he handed the phone back to the police officer.

"She wants to talk to you," he said, wiping his nose on his shirt sleeve.

Jennifer and Katy joined the small group. Jennifer asked Bobby if he was OK, and then turned her attention to Josh.

"Josh, I'm Bobby's mother. I'd like to help you. What can I do?"

After several deep breaths, Josh told her that his mother was coming home tonight. She had been working at a resort on the coast to try to earn enough money so they could move to Colorado and be near his grandparents. She had left him with her husband's brother for a week, and didn't realize what was going on.

Josh explained that his father had died a year ago and his mother was trying to support them on her own. She realized they needed more help and was planning to move to Colorado as soon as she had enough money for the trip.

"My mom's had a rough year," he said. "She's a very proud woman and doesn't like to ask for help, but she decided it would be better for both of us if we were near family. I didn't want to worry her, so I didn't tell her what Uncle Al was making me do." He started to cry again.

Jennifer put her arm around him as one of the police officers drove off with his uncle in the backseat of the police cruiser.

"Josh, you've had a rough day," Jennifer said in a calm voice. "But this is good news for you. You and your mother are going to get a new start in Colorado, and your uncle won't be bothering you anymore." She let that sink in before she continued.

"It sounds like you and your mother are very close," she said.

"Yes, we are. Especially since my dad died."

"I think you two are going to be fine," she said with confidence.

Josh was starting to breathe normally. Jennifer gave him a tissue to wipe his nose.

"Mom, can he spend the rest of the day with us?" Bobby asked.

Katy said, "Yeah, he can go with us to get some dessert."

"We have to catch the T in about an hour, but I think that's a great idea," Jennifer said. "I better talk to Josh's mother and see if it's OK with her."

The police officer who had been talking to Josh's mother on the phone thought that was a good idea too. He told her he'd see to it that Josh got home safely. And then he said to Jennifer, "I think spending some time with your kids for awhile will be just what he needs. They seem to have bonded."

"I should talk to Josh's mother as well," Jennifer said. "I want to make sure she's comfortable with letting Josh join us."

The police officer handed Jennifer the phone, and the two mothers had a friendly conversation.

"Josh's mother agreed to let him spend some time with us," Jennifer told the officer. "We had planned to visit this cemetery because the boys had read about it in *Johnny Tremain*, so I'll let them walk through it. Then we're heading over to Mike's Pastry to buy cannoli. My kids have never had them."

"They're in for a treat," the officer said. "I'll come over there in about an hour to get Josh. I need to go to the gift shop and make sure everything is OK there."

"Sounds like a plan," she replied.

"And Mrs. Johnson, your sons were instrumental in helping us catch this guy. If they hadn't acted so quickly, we would not have recovered the stolen wallet, nor been able to rescue Josh from his uncle. Who knows what would have happened to him? Your boys showed a lot of courage."

Joey and Bobby grinned at each other.

Bobby said, "Maybe we would have made good Patriots?"

"Maybe so," Joey replied proudly.

Chapter 17
Copp's Hill Burying Ground

The boys and Barby entered the old cemetery and were strolling along one of the brick walkways. Katy hesitated when her mother started up the stairs to the entrance.

"Mom, you know I don't like graveyards," she said. "Do we have to go in this one, too?"

"The boys wanted to come. I'd like to see some of the images on the gravestones. They're historic, and I might want to write a story on them someday," she said. "Let's look at a few. Then you and I will go back to the Old North Church gift shop and buy a cookbook for me and a picture book for you."

The cemetery sat atop a hill overlooking the harbor and sloped down toward a street below. Gray headstones lined up in long rows, many of them tilting at awkward angles. Some had jagged edges with pieces missing. Yellow daffodils bloomed along a few of the walkways and clustered around some of the graves between patches of green grass.

Jennifer pointed to a headstone that had a skull with wings at the top of the stone marker.

"That's scary looking," Katy said.

"Actually, that's a reflection of the time period," her mother told her. "It was the most common carving used in this graveyard in the late 1700s. It's an indication of how old these graves are."

Jennifer went on to explain that details like this help historians determine the age of something. Doing historical research can be like a good detective story, discovering clues about the thing's origins.

"Now, that should get Bobby's attention," Katy said with a laugh.

Bobby and Josh were looking for a headstone that had bullet holes in it because the British soldiers had used it for target practice when they occupied Boston prior to the American Revolution.

Joey and Barby had wandered to a different section, stopping to read many of the informational markers. They learned that Copp's Hill is the second-oldest cemetery in Boston, with several notable people buried there—like Robert Newman, the man who hung the lanterns in the steeple of the Old North Church, and the coppersmith who created the weathervane on top of Faneuil Hall.

Most of the graves belonged to merchants, craftsmen, and artisans.

"I remember that this is the place where Johnny Tremain's mother was buried," Joey said. "Did you ever read that book?"

"No, I haven't," Barby said. "But I will now."

They entered a grassy section that contained few gravestones. The informational marker indicated it was where many African Americans were buried. The marker noted that many Africans were brought to Boston in the 1600s and 1700s, in bondage as slaves to be sold in New England and in the southern colonies. However, some were able to secure their freedom, and a free African American community was established in the North End in 1650. In the 1780s slavery ended in Massachusetts.

"I didn't know that," Barby said. "I only knew about the Italians and Irish settling here. I'm glad you came to visit. I've learned a lot of new things today."

"I'm glad I came too," Joey said, and grabbed her hand. "Let's go check out that section. It says that they think more than a thousand African slaves, free African Americans, and even slave owners could be buried here."

They walked over to the designated area, but saw only a few headstones.

Barby said, "Oh! The marker said many of the headstones were removed or lost, or decayed because they were made out of wood."

They stood there for a moment, silently paying their respects to another group of courageous early settlers.

Their reverie was broken when Bobby yelled, "Hey, Joey, Mom's leaving. We gotta go."

"My grandmother says that Bobby's shouts could wake the dead," Joey said. "I hope that doesn't happen today."

Chapter 18
Cannoli for Everyone!

They walked back to the entrance, where Josh and Bobby were waiting for them.

"Mom and Katy went back to the gift shop to buy a book," Bobby said. "We're supposed to meet them there and then we're going to get cannoli. I still don't know what a cannoli is."

"You're going to love them," Barby said.

Josh agreed. "I've only had one once, but it sure was good."

Barby and Joey glanced at each other, realizing that Josh was in much better spirits. They fell in behind Bobby and Josh, who were doing a fast walk-run down Hull Street, racing to see who could get there first. Joey admitted to Barby that his brother actually had some good qualities.

"I like to hassle him—because that's what big brothers do—but when the going gets tough, we can count on Bobby," he said. "He really surprised me today when he charged out of the gift shop. I'm glad everything turned out OK."

"Everything turned out great!"Barby said."Don't forget that it was your photograph of Josh's uncle that helped too. I think you two make a good team."

When Jennifer and Katy came out of the gift shop, they were carrying white plastic bags containing several books.

"I bought each of you a book I thought you might like," Jennifer said.

"And I got a picture book and Mom got a cookbook," Katy said excitedly."Mom and I are going to make some of the recipes. I can't wait to show them to Grandma."

"I also bought a copy of *Johnny Tremain* for you, Josh," Jennifer said."I wasn't sure if you have read it. I thought it might be a nice souvenir of the time you spent with the Johnson family today."

Josh grinned broadly."Mrs. Johnson, I can guarantee you I will never forget your family."

"OK, then. Let's head over to Mike's Pastry. Cannoli for everyone!"Jennifer said.

They were only a few blocks from Mike's, but the streets and sidewalks were even more crowded than before. As they approached the Italian bakery, they noticed several people carrying white bakery boxes with blue lettering.

"Yep," Barby said, "they've all been to Mike's."

They entered the crowded shop as one of the small tables was being cleared. Barby rushed over to claim it so they'd have a place to sit down. There was only room for three chairs. Joey offered that he and Barby could go outside and Katy would have to sit on her mother's lap.

"Someone will come to wait on us, but you need to decide what you want," Barby said.

It was hard to see the pastries in the glass display cases with all the people waiting in line to make a purchase. Several of the staff worked at a brisk pace to serve the customers.

"I'll have one of everything," Bobby announced, peeking through the long line of people standing in front of one of the cases.

"You have to try the cannoli," Josh said. "And if I remember correctly, one is plenty big."

A waitress came to their table and asked for their order. Jennifer made a quick decision and suggested the waitress bring them a variety of six different kinds of cannoli.

"And I'll have a latte," she said to the waitress. She ordered water for the kids. "You kids won't need any extra sugar or caffeine. We still have a wedding to attend tonight."

The kids oohed and aahed when the cannoli arrived. Bobby claimed one with chocolate chips. Josh took one with chocolate drizzled on top. Katy went for the one with powdered sugar, and Barby suggested Joey try the one with sliced almonds dotting the cream oozing out of the tubular pastry.

"That's my favorite. It's the Florentine," she said.

"No, then you should have it," Joey said.

"I can come here anytime. You need to experience this while you're here."

Barby asked Jennifer which one she wanted. Jennifer said it didn't matter, but that the chocolate mousse was looking pretty good. Barby laughed and took the other one that was left.

She and Joey walked outside and found a place to sit on a curb a few doors down.

"I'm really glad your mother let me tag along today," Barby said. "I was afraid I wasn't going to be able to spend much time with you."

"Me too," Joey said. "I wish we were going to be here longer, but we have to fly back on Monday. I wish we could see each other again before we leave."

"Actually, that's going to happen," she said. "My dad bought tickets for all of us to go to the Red Sox game tomorrow. It's supposed to be a surprise, so don't let on that you know about it."

"You're kidding," Joey said excitedly. "My mom said she thought someone was taking care of getting us tickets, but I had no idea it was your dad."

"Yeah, she called him after she made your plane reservations. She knew you wanted to go to a game, and she thought it would be fun for our families to get together again. My parents really enjoyed the time we spent with your family when we visited St. Augustine last summer."

"I guess we're destined to reconnect periodically now that our families are friends," he said.

"I hope so," she replied.

Joey popped the last bite of his cannoli into his mouth and licked his fingers.

"We'll have to sit together at the game. That will give us a whole nine innings to chat," Joey said. "We've been so busy sight-seeing today, we really haven't had a chance to talk."

"I'd like that," she said.

Just then, Bobby came running up. "Hey, you two lovebirds," he said, "that police officer is here to take Josh home. You need to come and say bye."

Joey was annoyed with his brother's comment, but didn't have a good response so he said nothing. He and Barby walked back to where the others were standing. His mother and the officer were talking, while Josh was writing his mother's phone number on Bobby's arm.

"I don't have a phone of my own, and my mom says I'll get an email address when we get settled in Colorado."

"That's cool," Bobby said. "Let's stay in touch. You never know when I might have to make a business trip out West," he said with a chuckle.

Jennifer gave Josh her business card and asked him to give it to his mother.

"You tell her to call me and let me know how you're both doing. And let her know that you've got some friends in Florida if you'd ever like to come visit."

"Thank you, Mrs. Johnson," Josh said, and gave her a hug. "You and your family have helped me a lot."

Jennifer smiled and hugged him back. Katy, Joey, and Barby said their good-byes.

Bobby gave Josh a light punch on the arm and said, "Later, dude."

They walked away as the officer escorted Josh into a police car waiting nearby.

"Man, I wish I could ride in a squad car," Bobby said. "Now, that would make a good story."

"I think you've got a pretty good story to tell already," Joey said. "In fact, maybe I'll write an article about it and the headline will read 'Florida boy displays bravery in Boston.'"

"Yeah, me and Paul Revere," Bobby said proudly.

Chapter 19
Harvard Yard

They caught the T back to Harvard Square. They were thirty minutes early, before they were to meet Jennifer's relative who would drive them back to Kristina's house. Barby's father was going to pick her up after she called him.

"I'll give my dad a call. It will take him about thirty minutes to get here too," she said. "In the meantime, why don't we walk over to the Harvard campus? Harvard Yard is over there." She indicated its location with a nod.

They crossed Massachusetts Avenue and walked past several four-story brick buildings. They passed by students hurrying in different directions. Some were loaded with backpacks and laptops, while other zipped past on bicycles.

"This place looks old," Bobby said.

"It is old," Jennifer said. "I took a walking tour here years ago. This is the oldest institution of higher education in the United States. It was started shortly after the Pilgrims arrived at Plymouth Rock."

"No wonder the buildings look so old," Katy said.

"These buildings aren't that old. All of these buildings have been built over the years. However, the school does have some interesting history."

They came to an open grassy area crisscrossed with sidewalks. The trees that dotted the courtyard were beginning to show signs of green. Jennifer told the kids that sheep and cattle used to graze there. During the American Revolution, students were sent home so the buildings could be used in the war effort, she explained.

"Many think it was part of the Underground Railroad during the Civil War, helping African slaves escape to freedom. One of the buildings here has a trap door and a secret passageway to a hidden room," she said.

"Whoa," Bobby said. "This town is full of mystery and intrigue. Can we go see it?"

"We won't have time today," his mother replied. "What you need to appreciate is what a prestigious college this is. Eight American presidents earned degrees here. I wish we had enough time to visit some of the museums, but that will have to wait. We need to get back."

She suggested they walk back to the Square through the much-photographed Johnston Gate and she would take their picture there.

"There's a legend that says if you kiss your college sweetheart under the gate, you will spend the rest of your lives together," Barby said.

"Kissy, kissy," Bobby said. "Why don't you give Barby a smackeroo?"

Joey blushed and gave his brother a shove.

Joey said, "It's for students who go to college here, you bozo."

"I was only trying to help you out, big brother," Bobby replied.

Jennifer said, "Bobby, why don't you hold Katy's hand, and leave your brother alone."

A relieved Joey walked quietly beside Barby. "I have to apologize for my brother. Sometimes he is a smart aleck. I hope he didn't embarrass you."

"He didn't embarrass me. I brought it up because I thought it was a good idea," she said.

Joey stopped in his tracks. He checked to make sure his mother, sister, and brother, who were ahead of them, weren't looking. Then he leaned over and gave her a kiss on the cheek.

"Another historic moment in the city of Boston," she said, and tossed her head back, raised a fist in the air, and yelled "Yes!"

Chapter 20
Family Values

When they got back to Kristina's house, several relatives were helping to put final touches on the flower centerpieces for the tables at their cousin's wedding reception. The sweet smell of flowers hung in the air. Sarah was making bows out of lavender ribbon.

"Can I help make some bows?" Katy asked her cousin.

"Sure. I could use another pair of hands," Sarah said, and made a place for Katy to sit next to her at the kitchen table.

"I should have stayed and helped you today instead of traipsing off to the city," Jennifer said. "I assumed all of the flowers would be done by a florist."

"You did the right thing by taking your kids into Boston," Kristina said. "This is an old family tradition. We like to do the flowers ourselves for the family receptions."

"We're even using some of the flowers from our own gardens," Kristina's mother said. "It adds a nice touch, don't you think?"

"It's wonderful," Jennifer said. "How can I help?"

"You can help us load these into my SUV so I can deliver them to the women's club for the reception. Both the church and the club are a few minutes from here," Kristina said. "How was your day in Boston? Did the kids have a good time?"

"Actually, it turned into a bit of an adventure," Jennifer said. "I'll tell you about it as we load the car. Then I need to start getting these kids cleaned up and dressed, or we're going to be late for the wedding."

"If you really want to help, you can supervise my boys getting ready too," Kristina said. "After they get dressed, they can play some video games until it's time to leave. I'll be back shortly, and then I need to get dressed."

Kristina left, as did her mother and Sarah, and the other women who had been helping.

Joey and Bobby changed into their Sunday clothes, and went to the game room to join their cousins who were already dressed.

"Don't get dirty or wrinkled," Jennifer said to all of them. "We're going to be leaving shortly."

She helped Katy put on her favorite pink dress, and braided some of the lavender ribbon from the bows into her hair.

"I've never been to a wedding before," Katy said. "I can't wait to see the bride. I bet she'll look like a princess."

"I think you look like a princess," Jennifer said, and gave her a quick hug.

An hour later, they were all dressed and ready to go. Because there were eight of them, they had to take two cars. The four boys rode with Kristina's husband, Dave; and Jennifer, Kristina, and Katy rode together. They arrived at the church at the same time, along with many other guests.

The wedding was held in a historic white wooden church. It had a wide front porch, black shutters on the clear windows, and a tall church steeple with a clock.

"Do all churches here look like the Old North Church?" Bobby asked.

"No, not all of them," Dave said. "A lot of our churches have modern buildings, but many people like to use these historic structures for special events like weddings. This one even has a bell in the tower that they'll ring when the bride and groom are leaving the church."

"That will be cool," Joey said. "I wonder if Paul Revere made the bell. He seems to have made so many other things in this state."

Katy was delighted when the bride winked at her while walking down the aisle, going toward the front of the church. Jennifer and Kristina both sniffled when the minister pronounced the bride and groom "man and wife." The younger boys snickered when the couple kissed. The wedding was "short but beautiful," according to Katy.

They drove for a few minutes, to the women's club, which was decorated in lavender and had Sarah and Katy's ribbons festooned on the tables. A special table had been reserved for the kids, which included Sarah and her brother, Timothy. A bottle of sparkling grape juice was on their table, so they could also toast the bride and groom with the adults, who had champagne.

After dinner was served, a small band began playing music and several couples started dancing.

"C'mon, Joey," Sarah said. "Let's show these old folks how to dance."

"I can't dance," Joey said in a panic.

"Sure you can," she said. "There's nothing to it," and she grabbed his hand and pulled him onto the dance floor.

Bobby, David, Alan, and Timothy watched in surprise as Sarah coached Joey on the latest dance moves. Katy giggled and clapped her hands.

"Bobby, will you dance with me?" she said.

"There's no way I'm going out on that dance floor and make a fool of myself," he said.

"I'll dance with you," David said, and escorted Katy to the dance floor.

Neither one of them knew exactly what to do, but they had a good time swaying to the music. A photographer who had been taking pictures throughout the evening, took several photos of the kids dancing.

When the music stopped, Katy curtsied and David bowed to her. Joey patted Katy on the head as they all walked back to the table. He expected Bobby and Alan to make fun of them, but not a word was said.

"That was kind of fun," Joey said. "Dancing isn't as hard as I thought it would be."

"Like anything, the first time is the hardest," Sarah said. "Sometimes you gotta take a chance and go for it."

"I know what you mean," Joey said. "It's been a day of 'firsts' for me."

After the wedding cake was cut and the father of the bride danced with his daughter, Jennifer announced it was time for them to go home. Katy protested, but was also having a hard time staying awake.

"We had a busy day today, and we've got plans for tomorrow," Jennifer said. "We need a good night's sleep."

"I'm too excited to sleep," Katy said, but she fell asleep in the car on the way back to Kristina's house.

YAZ

Chapter 21
Baseball and Barby

The next day Kristina made blueberry pancakes for breakfast. Her husband and sons were going to join Jennifer's family in going to a Red Sox game that afternoon. Kristina was going to stay and help clean up after the wedding.

"I talked with Mr. Mason, Barby's dad, last week, and he's reserved tickets for us so we can sit with his family," Jennifer said. "They're going to join us at the game. We can pick up our tickets at Will Call."

Bobby asked, "What's Will Call?"

"That's a ticket window that you go to when you pick up tickets that have been ordered online or over the phone," Dave said. "I ordered some tickets too, but I don't think we'll be sitting together. If they haven't sold out for today's game, then we might be able to find seats near each other."

"I don't care where we sit, as long as it's in the ballpark," Joey said. "I've always wanted to go to Fenway."

Dave explained that because parking would be a challenge, they'd leave early. "The game starts at one thirty-five, but we want to get there in plenty of time to pick up our tickets and find our seats before the game starts."

"I'm ready," Joey said. "Let's go!"

"Hold your horses, son," Dave said. "We'll leave in thirty minutes."

"He's excited because he's got a hot date," Bobby said.

"Well then, we'll make it fifteen," Dave said with a wink. "I don't want to get in the way of a little romance."

Joey blushed and gave his brother a shove. "Why do you have to be such a jerk?"

Jennifer separated them and instructed them to go upstairs for their jackets. "In case it rains or gets chilly," she said.

Soon they were buckled into the SUV and on their way to Fenway. As they got closer to the ballpark, they found themselves in heavy traffic. Almost all the cars had some kind of Red Sox logo on their car, or around their license tag, and on the clothes of the passengers.

"I'm going to buy a new baseball cap," Joey said. "I have one, but it's old and I want one that I bought at Fenway."

"You need to buy a Fenway Frank too," Alan said.

"What's that?" Bobby asked.

"It's a hot dog, but we like to think it's kind of special," David said. "You can't go to Fenway and not eat a Fenway Frank."

"I wanna get some popcorn," Katy said. "And maybe Cracker Jacks. You can't go to a ball game and not get popcorn."

Dave drove to a parking lot that they liked to use on game days. He explained that they'd have to walk some distance, but he said they'd have lots of interesting things to see along the way.

They joined crowds of people who had ridden the T and were all walking in the same direction. Almost everyone had on some kind of red-and-blue Red Sox clothing. Some were cheering, "Let's go, Red Sox." Only a few people were wearing jerseys for the other team.

When the Johnsons and their relatives looked down Lansdowne Street, they caught sight of the tall light poles, the brick building with green trim, and the back of the huge video screen in center field proclaiming "Fenway Park, Home of the Boston Red Sox." Dave directed them to continue to Yawkey Way to go to the Will Call window for their tickets.

"Everybody stay together," Dave said. "It's going to get crowded. Someone hold on to Katy."

Hundreds of baseball fans were swarming in the street. A banner draped across the road stated "Welcome to Yawkey Way," with the famous logo depicting two red socks in the right corner. Delicious smells were coming from the many vendors selling food from stalls that backed up against the stadium wall. A large blue-and-red awning identified the Red Sox Team Store on the opposite side of the street.

"Mom, can we go in there?" Joey begged.

"Joey, let's get our tickets first," Dave said. "Then we can visit the store. But I'm warning you, it's going to be a madhouse in there."

"I don't care," Joey said. "I want to get a new cap."

"It might be less crowded after the game," Dave said.

They pushed through the crowds, trying to get to Gate D. Waiting there for them was the Mason family. Barby waved frantically with both arms so they would see them.

"We knew you'd have to come here to get your tickets, so we figured we'd wait here for you," Mr. Mason said.

Mrs. Mason gave Jennifer a hug. "It's so good to see you again. I'm glad we're able to share our city with you. You were so helpful to us when we visited Florida."

Katy rekindled her friendship with Laurie, Barby's little sister. They had become quick friends last summer when her family was visiting in St. Augustine.

And Barby sidled over to Joey, saying, "Hey, guy, did'ja miss me?"

Joey grinned. He was getting used to all this attention he was getting from her … and he liked it!

"I'll wait in line with Jennifer, to pick up the tickets," Dave said. "Why don't you take the kids around the corner to see the statues of some of the famous players?"

"That's a great idea," Mr. Mason said.

He led them to the Van Ness Street side of the stadium. A bronze statue of four players, titled "Teammates," depicting Ted Williams, Dom DiMaggio, Bobby Doerr, and Johnny Pesky, was the center of attention for dozens of fans. Another statue immortalized Ted Williams placing a baseball cap on a young boy's head.

"This is my favorite," Joey said, pointing to the statue titled "Yaz," of Carl Yastrzemski tipping his cap in the air. "He was considered by many to be the greatest left fielder ever. He played for the Red Sox for twenty-three years."

Barby said, "You really know your baseball, don't you?"

"I know about the Red Sox," he said.

"Then what are we waiting for? Let's go see 'em in action," she replied.

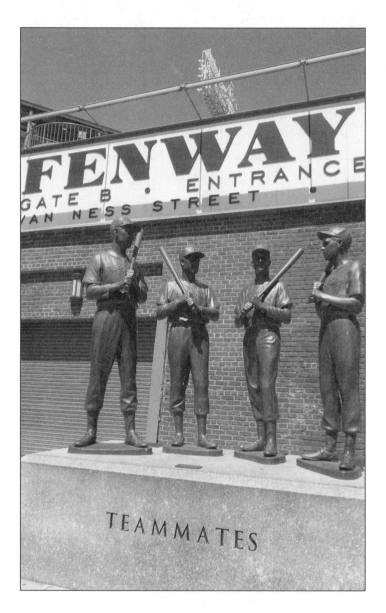

Chapter 22
A Day at Fenway

As they entered the famous stadium, Joey said he could hardly wait to see the Green Monster.

"A monster?" Katy said with surprise. "They have a monster here?"

"Yeah, it's a big green monster that likes to eat little girls, especially blond ones," Bobby teased.

Katy looked at Bobby with disgust. "I don't believe you."

"Good for you, Katy," Joey said. "Bobby's just being his obnoxious self. The Green Monster is a section of the left outfield wall that's painted green. It's famous for preventing home runs because it's more than thirty-seven feet high. I'll show it to you when we get in."

Soon they were caught up in a wave of excited sports fans, all eager to get inside. Mr. Mason explained that their seats were located on the first base side. As they got their initial glimpse of the field, Joey stopped in his tracks to take it all in.

"I can't believe I'm here," he said to Barby. "It's much bigger than I expected. I knew this was one of the oldest ballparks in the country, so I expected it to be smaller ... and old looking."

"There's nothing old about the video screen in center field," Barby said. "However, the scoreboard is still done the old-fashioned way, with people manually changing the numbers. It's part of the much-loved traditions that are maintained here at Fenway."

They found their seats in a section behind the Red Sox dugout and were surprised to see they were only a few rows away from Dave, David, and Alan. Katy and Laurie

wanted to sit together, as did Joey and Barby. Mrs. Mason and Jennifer sat next to each other, so Mr. Mason said he and Bobby would have to keep each other company.

"That's fine with me," Bobby said. "There's too much girl talk going on here, and I don't think my brother is going to pay too much attention to me today."

Mr. Mason agreed. "We can talk some serious baseball. I'll buy a program and we can keep score."

Players from both teams were on the field warming up. Many fans gathered around the dugouts, hoping to get an autograph. Joey was pointing out the players he recognized. He took lots of pictures of the players and the ballpark.

"I still can't believe I'm really here," he said. "This is a perfect ending to our visit."

"Hopefully it won't be your last visit here," Barby said.

"Me too," Joey said. "I'll have to make it an annual trip."

"I hope you do," she said.

Mr. Mason bought the adults and the older kids Fenway Franks; Katy and Laurie opted for pizza. Joey asked them all to pose while taking a bite of their hot dog and pizza, so he could take a picture of them. He then took several shots of Barby, who smiled up at him sweetly. Joey's mother offered to take a photo of the two of them together, knowing Joey would want to have that later.

Soon the players returned to their dugouts, and a blond woman with an opera-like voice sang the national anthem. The home plate umpire called "Play ball," and the crowd cheered as the first batter stepped to the plate.

Neither team scored until the third inning, when the Red Sox loaded the bases. A double hit to center field scored two runs. That fired up the Sox fans, until the opposing team tied the game in the top of the fifth inning with a two-run homer.

There was a break in the action as the Red Sox manager brought in a new pitcher. Bobby and Mr. Mason went to buy popcorn for everyone. Joey and Barby talked about their schools, what kinds of books they liked to read, their favorite movies, and what they planned to do over the summer. Barby said she hoped her family would be going to Florida again, but she didn't think that would happen.

"I guess we'll have to stay in touch by email," Joey said. "And we can Skype."

"I'd like that," Barby said. "I'd like to stay in touch."

The game resumed, but neither team scored for the next three innings, the opposing pitchers not allowing any additional runs.

In the middle of the eighth inning everyone stood up to sing "Sweet Caroline," a Fenway tradition.

"That was so cool," Bobby said. "I'm becoming a Red Sox fan too. I wanna get a baseball cap before we leave."

"We can stop at the team store across the street on our way out," Mr. Mason said. "They have all kinds of caps, T-shirts, jerseys, and souvenirs."

Just then, a foul ball was hit into the stands.

Joey yelled, "Heads up!" when he saw it coming in their direction.

A fan three rows in front of them caught the ball. His friends patted him on the back as the crowd applauded.

"Man, I wish I had caught that," Bobby said. "That would be the best souvenir ever."

The Red Sox got a runner on base in the eighth inning, but failed to score. Neither did the opposing team at the top of the ninth. Two Boston players struck out in the bottom of the ninth. As the next batter came to the plate, the hometown crowd was standing and cheering for their team.

Joey and Barby joined in, cheering, "Let's go, Red Sox!"

The batter swung at the first pitch and sent the ball sailing over the Green Monster, scoring the winning run. Everyone was jumping up and down, giving high fives, and hugging the people next to them … including Joey and Barby.

"That was a perfect ending to this game," Joey said. "I'm so glad he hit it to left field. I'll never forget this day."

"Me too," Barby said. "I hope we can come here together again someday."

"You can count on it," Joey said. "I'll definitely be back."

Chapter 23
Saying Good-bye

They joined up with Dave, Alan, and David, and asked if they could visit the Red Sox Team Store before they left. It was total chaos on Yawkey Way, the street between the ballpark and the team store, as hundreds of Boston fans were celebrating their victory.

Jennifer warned her kids to stay together. Unfortunately, she was too late. Bobby was nowhere in sight.

"Has anyone seen Bobby?" she said with concern.

Joey said, "He was right behind us a minute ago."

Jennifer looked panic-stricken. "We need to find a police officer right away. There are hundreds of people here. We'll never find him," she said.

"He knows we're going to the store, so I'm sure he'll head that way," Mr. Mason said. "The rest of you go to the store. Dave and I will go look for him."

"I'll go too," Joey said to his mother. "I'll be OK. I'll stay with them. I need to go find him."

"Stay with the adults. I don't need two of you lost," Jennifer said with a shaky voice.

The three of them pushed through the rowdy crowd, calling Bobby's name. Because the street was closed off to car traffic, they walked down the middle of the road, looking to their left and right.

"Wait a minute," Joey said. "Mom told us if we ever got lost, to go to the place where we were last together. That would be right outside the gate we came out from. He was right behind us when we left the park."

They turned around and walked back to that gate. Leaning against the wall and holding onto his program was a forlorn-looking Bobby. His face lit up when he saw Joey coming toward him.

"Am I glad to see you," Bobby said.

"Yeah, me too," Joey replied. "What happened to you?"

"I dropped my program and bent down to pick it up, and when I looked up, all of you were gone. There were so many people everywhere and I couldn't see which direction you had gone, so I decided to stay put. I was hoping you'd come back here."

"That was smart of both of you to remember that," Dave said. "I'll give your mother a call on her cell phone, and then let's join the others and calm down a very nervous mother."

126

Jennifer was standing outside the store, searching the crowd nervously for some familiar faces. When she saw them returning with Bobby in tow, she let out a deep breath of relief.

"Are you OK?" she said. "You scared me to death! Don't ever do that again."

"I'm fine," Bobby said. "I didn't mean to scare you. I'm sorry." And then he added, "Can I still get a baseball cap?"

She hesitated for a moment, but then smiled and said, "Of course. Just stay where I can see you."

They entered the huge store that was full of all kinds of Red Sox merchandise.

Joey said, "This looks like the mall at Christmastime."

"It's always like this on game days," Dave said.

"Where are the girls?" Joey asked his mother.

"Barby took them to the kids' clothing section. I told Katy I'd buy her something."

"Good," he replied. "I'd like to buy something for Barby, but I don't want her to see it. Why don't you take Bobby over to the baseball cap section. I'll join you there in a minute. I want to get a new cap too."

Joey wandered through several of the aisles, trying to find something appropriate for Barby. Then he spotted the perfect item. After he made his purchase, he joined his mother and brother, and he and Bobby both bought new caps. Bobby selected a red one and Joey picked a blue one, so they wouldn't get them mixed up.

Katy found a pink hoodie that she wanted, and Laurie's mother bought Laurie one to match. Before Jennifer got in line to pay, she told her kids they would be leaving shortly so they needed to say their good-byes to the Masons.

Joey and Barby drifted away from the others. They were both silent, feeling awkward and not knowing what to say.

"I'm glad you came to Boston," Barby said.

"Me too," Joey mumbled. "I'm really glad you went with us yesterday and that we were able to come here together today. That made it all extra special."

"It was special for me too," she said.

"I wanted to give you something to remember today," he said. He handed her a white plastic bag with the Red Sox logo on it. "I bought this for you. I hope you'll think of me when you look at it."

She opened the bag and pulled out a caramel-colored stuffed bear with a red bow tied around its neck. It was wearing a Red Sox T-shirt. She hugged it, and then hugged Joey.

"Thank you," she said. "I love it! It makes me smile when I look at it … and I will think of you."

"Good, I like to think of you smiling."

"OK, troops. Time to go," Dave said. "Hopefully the traffic will have cleared out a little."

Because the Masons had parked their car in the other direction, they said good-bye outside the store. Jennifer hugged Laurie, Barby, and Mrs. Mason. She thanked Mr. Mason again for their tickets.

"This was a treat for all of us," she said. "I hope you'll visit Florida again and let us return the favor."

"It was our pleasure," Mr. Mason said. "We all had a good time."

Katy and Laurie had both put on their new pink hoodies. They giggled and twirled around like fashion models. Bobby was wearing his new cap and said he was even going to sleep in it. Barby had put the teddy bear back in its bag, but she was clutching it tightly in her arms.

"I guess this is good-bye," Joey said. He shook hands with Mr. Mason and thanked him again for the tickets. He gave Mrs. Mason a hug, and patted Laurie on the head. He turned to Barby, who looked solemn.

"I'm glad I got some good pictures of you earlier, when you were smiling," he said.

She brightened up and gave him a brief grin. "I hate good-byes," she said.

"Me too, but I'm sure we're going to see each other again," he said.

"Promise?" she asked.

"Promise!" he said, and stepped closer to give her a hug.

"Let's go, Romeo," Bobby teased.

Jennifer grabbed the neck of Bobby's shirt and pulled him away. "We'll start walking to the car. You can catch up with us," she said to Joey. She gave a final wave to the Masons, who then started to walk in the other direction.

Joey took hold of Barby's hand and said he'd call her later. She looked at him, and threw her arms around him and briefly hugged him tight. She kissed him on the cheek and turned and walked away quickly.

Joey stared after her, sad and frustrated. *Why didn't I say more?* he thought. *I'm not used to being serious with a girl.*

She turned around and yelled at him, holding up the bear: "Hey, Johnson, I'm going to name him Joey Jr. So if your ears start burning, you'll know we're talking about you."

Joey laughed and gave her a thumbs-up. He waved one last time and then turned to join his family.

Chapter 24
Home Again

Their last night at Kristina and Dave's house was noisy and full of laughter. The younger boys were recapping the baseball game for Kristina, each trying to outdo the others with play-by-play details.

Joey was asking Dave about some of the sports they played in Massachusetts that they didn't have in Florida. Katy was looking through some of the old family photographs, pointing to faces and asking her mother to identify them.

"Are we related to all these people?" she asked.

"Most of them," Jennifer said. "I'm glad someone wrote the names on the back of many of these pictures, or I wouldn't know who they are."

"Their clothes are so old-fashioned, and most of them never seem to smile. Were they unhappy?"

"I don't think so," Jennifer replied. "That was the way they posed for pictures back then."

"I like the way we do things today," Katy said. "But it's kinda fun to see the way people used to look and how they lived. I can't wait to tell my teacher about all the things we saw this weekend."

"I'm glad you liked it," Jennifer said.

Kristina set out a plate of fresh-baked snickerdoodles and poured five glasses of milk.

"Here's a little snack before bedtime," she said. "My boys need to get to bed. They have school in the morning."

"My kids need to turn in too. It's been a busy few days. What time should we leave for the airport tomorrow?" Jennifer asked.

"We better be on the road by ten. Hopefully the traffic won't be too bad," Kristina said.

"Mom, can Alan and David come visit us in Florida sometime?" Bobby said. "We could take them to the beach, and to St. Augustine, and to Disney World, and—"

"Of course they can," she said, "but you better check with their parents first. The invitation is always open."

Dave responded by saying, "I think we can put that on a list of places we'd like to visit."

His response was greeted with cheers from the boys. As they finished their cookies and milk, they started making plans for a future vacation.

"I'm glad the kids got along so well," Kristina said. "It's sad that we live so far away from many of our relatives. You'll just have to come back again someday."

"We will do that," Jennifer said. "But for now, we need to get these kids to bed. It's going to be another long day tomorrow."

The boys made a competition about who could get ready for bed the fastest. Katy complained that she wasn't as fast as the older kids, so she wasn't going to participate in their silly game. Joey was not interested in racing either. He had been fairly quiet throughout the evening.

"Are you OK?" Jennifer asked him, after the others raced up the stairs.

"Sure," he replied. "I'm just thinking about all the things we saw, the places we visited, and the people we met."

"Are you thinking about one person in particular?" she asked.

He was quiet for a moment, and then said, "Yeah. I'm glad we came, and I'm glad I got to spend time with Barby again. It went by so fast."

Jennifer put an arm around her son. "There can be other trips, and you can stay in touch with each other through email and on cell phones. But remember that you've got high school and college ahead. You'll be meeting other girls

133

and she'll meet other boys. That's all part of growing up, and neither of you should miss out on that."

He wasn't very happy with that thought.

"Both of you should think of each other as good friends. And then someday when you're older, if your relationship becomes more serious, you won't have any regrets."

"Yeah, I know you're right," he said. "It's easier said than done."

She patted him on the back and said, "Welcome to the real world, Joey."

When their plane took off the next day, Bobby was reading the new book his mother had bought for him at the Old North Church gift shop. Katy was holding Winnie-the-Pooh up to the window so he could see the Boston skyline.

Joey was thinking about all the things that had happened to him over the past five days. He got to know new relatives he'd never met before; he visited some historic places he had only read about in books; he helped capture a criminal; he attended a Red Sox game at Fenway Park, a longtime dream of his; he learned to dance with a girl; and he got kissed ... twice!

Bobby asked, "What are you smiling about, Joey?"

"I was just remembering what a fun trip it's been," he said.

"Yeah, I liked it too," Bobby said. "I hope we can come back again someday."

"I plan to do that," Joey said. *I definitely plan to do that,* he thought as the plane headed back to Florida.

THE END

Resources

Old North Church
193 Salem Street
Boston, MA 02113
(617) 523-6676
www.oldnorth.com

Paul Revere House
19 North Square
Boston, MA 02113
(617) 523-2338
www.paulreverehouse.org

USS *Constitution*
Charlestown Navy Yard
Building 5
Charlestown, MA 02129
www.history.navy.mil/ussconstitution

USS Constitution Museum
Charlestown Navy Yard
Building 22
Charlestown, MA 02129
(617) 426-1812
www.ussconstitutionmuseum.org

Other Books by Jane R. Wood

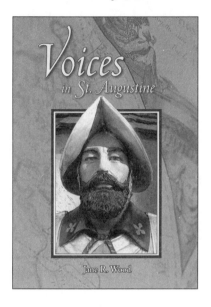

Voices in St. Augustine

Thirteen-year-old Joey Johnson has a problem. He hears voices, only he can't find the people who belong to them. His curiosity leads him on a quest where he learns more than just history about the Nation's Oldest City.

Mom's Choice Awards®
Silver Recipient

Price: $8.99

140 Pages

ISBN: 978-0-9792304-5-5

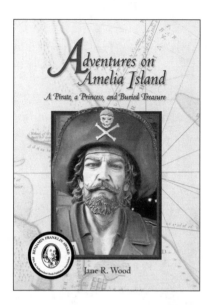

Adventures on Amelia Island:
A Pirate, a Princess, and Buried Treasure

This book continues the escapades of the Johnson family. Local legends and tales of ghosts add to a story filled with colorful characters, humorous situations, and a youthful spirit of adventure.

Benjamin Franklin Award
Silver Recipient

Mom's Choice Awards®
Silver Recipient

Accelerated Reader™

Price: $8.99

163 Pages

ISBN: 978-0-9792304-6-2

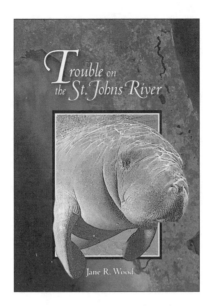

Trouble on the St. Johns River

After a close encounter with a manatee, a visit to a sea turtle center, and a family river tour, Joey, Bobby, and Katy decide to "do something" to try to make a difference in protecting endangered animals and preserving the environment.

Mom's Choice Awards®
Silver Recipient

Accelerated Reader™

Price: $8.99

156 Pages

ISBN: 978-0-9792304-4-8

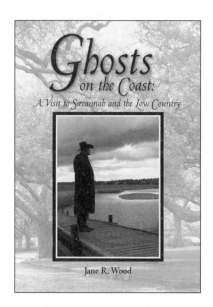

Ghosts on the Coast:
A Visit to Savannah and the Low Country

It seems wherever they go, adventure follows the Johnson family. This time it comes when they visit the historic cities of Savannah, Charleston, and Pawleys Island, South Carolina—cities rich in history and ghost stories!

Mom's Choice Awards®
Silver Recipient

Price: $8.99

132 Pages

ISBN: 978-0-9792304-0-0

All of Jane R. Wood's books may be ordered through

www.janewoodbooks.com.

About the Author

Jane R. Wood was born in Astoria, Oregon, and moved to Florida with her family when she was ten. She received a BA degree from the University of Florida and her MEd from the University of North Florida. She is a former teacher, newspaper reporter, and television producer. *Lost in Boston* is the fifth book in the series that chronicles the adventures of the Johnson family. Mrs. Wood likes to select historic locations for the settings of her books, and weave history into stories packed with mystery, adventure, and fun.

Jane Wood has two grown sons and three grandchildren, and lives in Jacksonville, Florida, with her husband Terry.

You can visit her website at www.janewoodbooks.com.